Ven

Rattlers
and Other Snakes

Concept and Product Development: Editorial Options, Inc.
Series Designer: Karen Donica
Book Author: Cecilia Venn

**For information on other World Book
products, visit us at our Web site at**
http://www.worldbook.com

**For information on sales to schools and libraries
in the United States, call 1-800-975-3250.**

**For information on sales to schools and libraries
in Canada, call 1-800-837-5365.**

World Book, Inc.
233 N. Michigan Ave.
Chicago, IL 60601

Library of Congress Cataloging-in-Publication Data

Venn, Cecilia.
    Rattlers and other snakes / [book author, Cecilia Venn].
        p. cm.—(World Book's animals of the world)
    Summary: Questions and answers explore the world of snakes, with an emphasis on rattlesnakes.
    ISBN 0-7166-1204-6 -- ISBN 0-7166-1200-3 (set)
    1. Rattlesnakes—Juvenile literature. 2. Snakes—Juvenile literature. [I. Rattlesnakes—
Miscellanea. 2. Snakes—Miscellanea. 3. Questions and answers.] I. World Book, Inc. II. Title.
III. Series.

QL666.069 V46 2000
597.96—dc21   00-021635

Printed in Singapore
1 2 3 4 5 6 7 8 9 05 04 03 02 01 00

World Book's Animals of the World

Rattlers
and Other Snakes

Why do I use a rattle?

World Book, Inc.
A Scott Fetzer Company
Chicago

Contents

Who can spit
the farthest?

Do you believe
I can fly?

What Is a Snake?

A snake is a long, legless animal that belongs to a group of animals called reptiles. Alligators, lizards, and turtles are all reptiles. Dinosaurs, which roamed the earth millions of years ago, were reptiles, too.

Like humans, reptiles are vertebrates, animals with backbones. Reptiles also breathe air through lungs. Unlike humans, reptiles have dry, scaly skin. They are also cold-blooded. This means that they do not have a steady body temperature, as humans do. Their body temperatures change with the temperature around them. Snakes lie in the sun to warm up or to raise their body temperatures. They crawl into the shade to cool off or to lower their body temperatures.

There are about 6,500 species, or kinds, of reptiles, including snakes. And there are lots and lots of different snakes—around 2,700 different species!

Red diamondback
rattlesnake

Where in the World Do Snakes Live?

Snakes live almost everywhere. You might see one while crossing a desert, climbing a mountain, or hiking in a forest. You might even see one while swimming in a lake, a river, or an ocean.

Even if you don't see snakes, they probably live near you. Snakes can live anyplace where the ground isn't frozen all year. They live on every continent, except Antarctica. (It is too cold and frozen!) A few islands—such as Ireland, Iceland, and New Zealand—are also snake-free.

Many snakes live on the ground. Others burrow under the ground. Some snakes like the high life and live in the trees. Still others like to stay wet and spend most of their lives in the water.

World Map

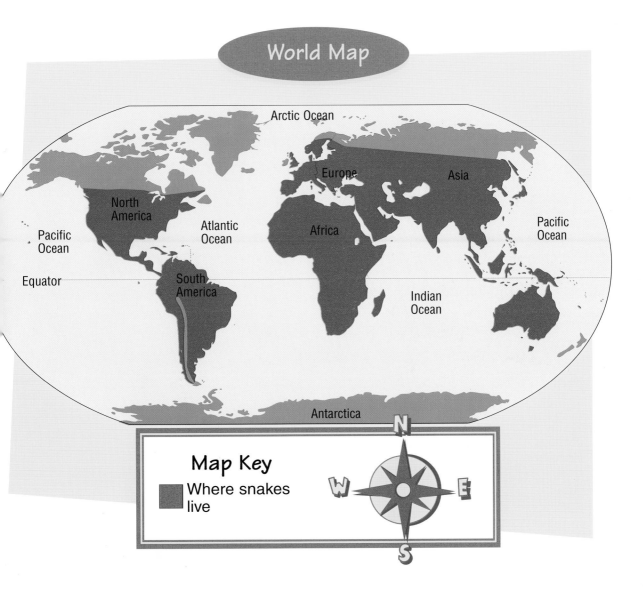

Arctic Ocean

Europe

Asia

North America

Atlantic Ocean

Africa

Pacific Ocean

Pacific Ocean

Equator

South America

Indian Ocean

Antarctica

Map Key

Where snakes live

N

W

E

S

9

Are Snakes Deadly or Harmless?

If you said deadly, you are right. If you said harmless, you are right, too! There are more than 400 species of poisonous snakes. But most of the world's snakes, almost 85 percent of the species, are harmless to people. Like these red-sided garter snakes, they are nonpoisonous. Australia is the only continent where you will find more poisonous than nonpoisonous snakes.

Most poisonous snakes belong to either of two families of snakes: elapids *(EHL uh pihdz)* and vipers *(VY puhrz)*. Elapids generally have short fangs. When elapids bite, they usually hang onto their prey. This gives their poisonous venom *(VEHN uhm)* more of a chance to enter the victim's body. Vipers strike quickly. Their long fangs deliver their venom deeply and quickly into their prey. One kind of viper you have probably heard about is the rattlesnake.

Red-sided garter
snakes

How Did the Rattlesnake Get Its Name?

Look! This snake is ready to strike. At the end of its tail is a hard, horny rattle. Listen! A dry, rattling *buzzzz* warns you to stay away! It is the rattle, and its warning sound gave the rattlesnake, or rattler, its name.

A rattlesnake's rattle is made up of rings of thick, dry scales that are loosely joined together. When a rattler shakes its tail, the rings rattle against one another. If you ever hear that sound, watch out!

Many people believe that they can tell the age of a rattlesnake by counting the rings in its rattle. But this is not true. Each time a rattlesnake sheds, a new ring is added to the base of the rattle. This means that rattlers may get two to four new rings a year. But rattlers also lose rings as the old ones at the tip of the rattle wear down and fall off.

Rattlesnake

Where Do Rattlesnakes Live?

Rattlesnakes inhabit the prairies, grasslands, pine woods, swamps, and forests of both North and South America. Their range reaches from southern Canada to Argentina. A few live east of the Mississippi River, but most live in southwestern United States and northern Mexico.

There are about 30 species of rattlesnakes. Some, like the ridge-nosed rattlesnake, usually grow between 15 and 24 inches (38 and 61 centimeters). Others, like the eastern diamondback rattlesnake, are long, thick, and heavy. Eastern diamondbacks are the longest rattlers. They grow to more than 7 feet (2.2 meters) in length!

Eastern diamondback rattlesnake

How Does Rattlesnake Skin Feel and Look?

If you just look at a snake, you may think it is wet and slimy. But this is not true. Rattlesnakes, like other snakes, have cool, dry, scaly skins.

Most snakes have scales that overlap and stretch apart. The patterns and colors on a snake come mainly from special color cells in the deep layers of a snake's skin. Brown, black, and yellow are common colors for rattlesnakes. These colors help rattlers blend in with their surroundings.

All snakes have two layers of skin—an inner layer of growing cells and an outer layer of dead cells. As snakes grow, they molt, or shed, the outer layer of skin. A snake begins to molt by rubbing loose the skin around its mouth and head. Then it crawls out of its skin!

Most rattlesnakes molt two to four times a year. Young snakes may shed more often because their bodies are growing more quickly.

Molting
rattlesnake

What Is Under All Those Scales?

Snakes have remarkable skeletons under their scaly skins. They have about 150 to over 430 vertebrae *(VUR tuh bray),* the small bones that make up a backbone. Humans have only 33! Each snake vertebra has a pair of ribs and as many as 24 small muscles attached to it. All these bones and muscles make it easy for a snake to bend around and around.

Snakes also have unusual bones in their heads. The jaw bones are only loosely attached to each other and to the rest of the snake's skull. This allows the two sides of a snake's mouth to move separately. It also lets a snake open its mouth wide enough to swallow a meal bigger than its head!

Most of a snake's inner organs are long and slender to fit inside its skeleton. But just like its mouth, a snake's stomach has to be able to handle big, bulky food. It has to really stretch to hold and digest a snake's meal.

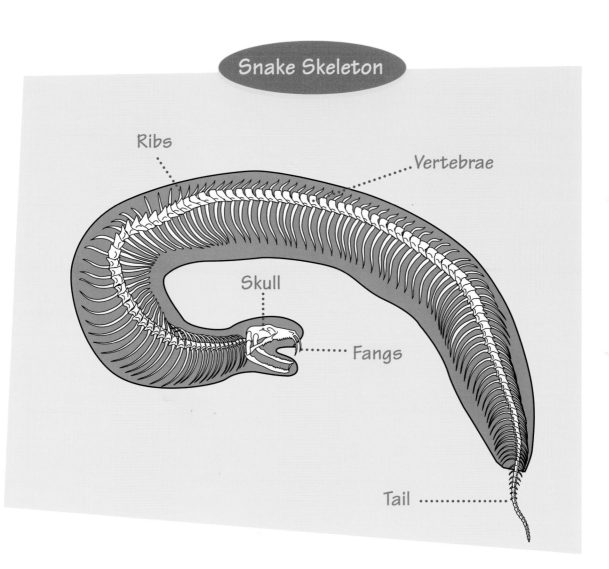

Snake Skeleton

Ribs

Vertebrae

Skull

Fangs

Tail

How Do Rattlesnakes Move?

Snakes have four main ways to travel. The most common is an S-shaped crawl. To do this, a snake wriggles from side to side, pushing against things so that it can move forward.

To climb trees, snakes push and pull their way. First, a snake coils and anchors the back half of its body and pushes the front half forward. Then the snake anchors the front half and pulls up the back half.

Sidewinding helps snakes cross hot desert sands. Here, a snake leaves its head and tail on the ground while it lifts and throws its body to the side. The snake then moves its head and tail in line with the body.

Snakes also move with a forward crawl. Stretching its body out in a straight line, a snake tightens and relaxes its muscles so that its scutes *(SKYOOTZ),* or belly scales, push and pull along the ground.

Sidewinder rattlesnake

How Do Rattlesnakes Find Their Prey?

Snakes have special sense organs to help them find their prey.

Look at this rattlesnake. With a flick of its tongue, it can tell if a tasty meal is near. The snake's tongue picks up animal smells from the air. The tongue then delivers the smells to a sense organ in the roof of the snake's mouth. This organ, called the Jacobson's organ, is very sensitive to smells. It works along with the snake's nose to help the snake follow an animal's scent.

Some snakes, like rattlesnakes, have another way of finding prey. These snakes have heat-sensing pit organs on the sides of their heads. All warm-blooded animals give off body heat. The pit organs sense this heat and help snakes track their prey.

Western diamondback
rattlesnake

What Are Fangs For?

Fangs are for biting, of course! Only poisonous snakes have fangs and venom glands. Fangs are hollow teeth connected to venom glands in a snake's upper jaw. When a snake bites an animal, the venom travels through the fangs to the bite.

Vipers, which include rattlesnakes, have long, movable front fangs. Their fangs spring forward for attack. They fold back on the roof of the mouth when not in use. Most other poisonous snakes have shorter fangs that do not move.

Snake venom is meant to kill an animal. Most venom has two kinds of poison. The poisons work together to damage an animal's nerves, heart, breathing, blood vessels, and body tissues. Venom also has special enzymes *(EN zymz)* in it that help a snake digest an animal more quickly!

Eastern diamondback rattlesnake

What Is a Clutch of Rattlers?

Female rattlesnakes give birth to live young. A group of newborn rattlers is called a clutch.

A mother rattler leaves her clutch shortly after the baby rattlers are born. Young rattlers can already care for themselves. They are able to find their own food. And they are already dangerous, because rattlesnakes are poisonous at birth.

Young rattlers, however, must still watch out for danger. Birds, animals, and even other snakes will swallow up baby rattlers.

Clutch of rattlesnakes

Who Is Hatching from That Egg?

Why, it is a baby snake! Unlike rattlesnakes, most species of snakes lay eggs. Depending on the species, a female snake may lay as few as 6 eggs or as many as 100 eggs at one time!

Snake eggs have leathery shells. The shells stretch as the baby snake inside grows. After several weeks, the baby snakes are ready to hatch. A hatching baby snake has a special tooth—an egg tooth—that tears open the shell so that it can wriggle out. Soon after hatching, the baby snake sheds this tooth.

Female snakes lay eggs in holes, burrows, rotten logs, tree stumps, and other such places. A few species of snakes, such as pythons, coil around their eggs to protect them and keep them warm. But most snakes leave their eggs after laying them. The eggs are left to hatch on their own. Some don't make it. The eggs are eaten by other animals.

Green tree python

Who's Who in the Snake World?

The world is home to some pretty amazing snakes. There are blind snakes that burrow underground and may be mistaken for worms. There are sea snakes that gracefully swim through the water.

Snakes also come in an amazing range of sizes. There are tiny Biminy *(BIHM uh nee)* blind snakes, which are only 6 inches (15 centimeters) long. And there are giant anacondas, which reach more than 30 feet (9 meters).

Some snakes even seem to fly! Flying snakes, such as this golden tree snake from Thailand, shoot out from tree limbs. They flatten their bodies to slow their fall.

Golden tree snake

What Does a Snake's Coloring Mean?

Bright colors—like the red, black, and yellow or white bands of a coral snake—mean danger. They warn animals that may try to eat the coral snake that this snake's bite is poisonous.

Some harmless snakes, such as scarlet kingsnakes and some milk snakes, mimic or copy the coloring of coral snakes. Their bright colors make them look dangerous to animals that prey on the snakes. A closer look, however, shows that the colored bands on these snakes appear in a different order.

Some snakes use their coloring as camouflage *(KAM uh flahzh)* to blend in with their surroundings. The green vine snake and other tree snakes loop themselves around tree branches. Hidden among the leaves, they look like vines. Their prey may not notice them—until it is too late!

Eastern coral snake

What's for Dinner?

It is easy to see what is on the menu for some snakes—eggs. For others, dinner depends on the species of snake and where it lives. Snakes eat almost any animal that fits into their bodies—fish, frogs, lizards, birds, small mammals—even other snakes!

Like many snakes, egg eaters can eat food that is bigger than their heads. A few egg-eating snakes, such as this African egg eater, have special features for eating eggs. Pointed spines on the neck bones break through the eggshell, allowing the snake to swallow the liquid inside. Then muscles in the snake's neck crush the shell, which is spit out. Other egg eaters, however, eat the whole egg—shell and all.

Snakes do not need to eat very often. One reason is that they don't need the food energy to make their own body heat. (Don't forget—snakes are cold-blooded!) The other reason is that snakes often eat big meals for their size, so they are not hungry again right away.

Egg-eating snake

Have You Seen This Snake in the Grass?

People in woodlands, fields, city parks, and backyards have been startled by this reptile. Garter, or "garden," snakes are very common. There are 13 different kinds of garter snakes in the United States alone, and most states have at least one kind.

These harmless snakes are usually easy to identify. Most garters have three stripes—one down their back and one down each side. Frogs, fish, and other cold-blooded animals are their main diet.

Garter snakes live throughout North and Central America. They have adapted to cold climates better than most snakes. In fact, the red-sided garter snake lives as far north as Canada's Northwest Territories. That is farther north than any other reptile in North America!

Northwestern garter snake

Why Do Copperheads Feel the Heat?

Copperheads are the pits! Pit vipers, that is. Like rattlesnakes, they can sense the body heat of other animals through small organs on either side of their heads. These deep pits can detect temperature changes as small as one degree.

Copperheads have something else in common with rattlesnakes. They are poisonous, and they kill animals with their venom. Copperheads do not have rattles, but young ones still use their tails. They wriggle their yellow-tipped tails to fool prey into coming closer. The yellow tips fade away as the snakes get older.

Copperheads have reddish-brown bands of color on their bodies. These bands make it hard to see copperheads among fallen leaves. In the United States, copperheads live in parts of New England, the Midwest, and the South.

Copperhead

What Makes the Kingsnake King?

A kingsnake's diet can include turtle eggs, birds, and small mammals. But what makes the kingsnake a king among North American snakes is that it eats other snakes—even poisonous rattlesnakes and copperheads! How can kingsnakes do this? They are not very affected by snake venom.

Kingsnakes are not poisonous. So how do they kill their prey? The kingsnake wraps around its prey and squeezes it to death.

Not all kingsnakes are alike. They may be brown or black. They may be speckled or have colored bands, rings, spots, or other patterns.

The common kingsnake is black with narrow yellow bands across its body. It grows to about 3 1/2 feet (107 centimeters). The prairie kingsnake is a light brownish color with black-edged brown or greenish blotches.

Speckled kingsnake

41

Why Do Milk Snakes Hang Around Barns?

A slender snake silently enters a barn. Is the snake there to drink a cow's milk? No, but that's what people once believed. The milk snake is really looking for a mouse or a rat. If there isn't one, a lizard or a small bird will do.

A milk snake is a kind of kingsnake. And there are many different kinds of milk snakes. Some may grow as long as 6 feet (1.8 meters). None are poisonous.

Like the kingsnake, milk snakes come in different colors and patterns. The eastern milk snake is gray with brownish spots on its back and sides. Some kinds are brightly colored. Their red, black, and yellow bands make them look like coral snakes. Coral snakes are deadly—which is why a lot of milk snakes end up dead. People often mistake them for coral snakes and kill them.

Eastern milk snake

What Is Wide-Mouthed, Dangerous, and Swims?

The answer is a cottonmouth. Cottonmouths look alarming when they are alarmed. They throw back their heads and gape, showing the cotton-white linings of their mouths. A gaping mouth is a warning to stay away. And so you should! These vipers are very poisonous.

Cottonmouths, also called water moccasins, live in the streams, swamps, lakes, and wetlands in the southeastern part of the United States. Of all the pit vipers, cottonmouths are the only ones normally found in water. They are excellent swimmers, gliding through the water with their heads raised. Fish, frogs, birds, small mammals, and even baby alligators can be part of their diet.

Cottonmouths have dark bodies. Some kinds are also marked with darker crossbands. They are about 3 1/2 feet (1 meter) long but may grow to 5 feet (1.5 meters).

Cottonmouth

When Does a Hognose Snake Fake?

When a hognose snake is afraid, it tries to fool its attacker by pretending, or faking, to be something it's not.

When faking an enemy, a hognose snake first puffs up its head and body. (This practice earned it the nickname "blowing adder.") It then hisses. It may also pretend to strike, but with its mouth closed.

If the enemy does not leave, the snake pulls another fake. It rolls over and plays dead. It throws back its head and lets its tongue hang out. Many predators will not eat dead food, so they leave the hognose alone. When the predator is gone, the hognose stops playing dead.

Hognose snakes live across much of the United States. Their blunt snouts help them dig up food such as toads. Hognoses have a mild venom that is poisonous to toads. But the bite of a hognose snake will not kill people.

Eastern hognose

Are Racer Snakes Fast?

Yes, they are—for snakes that is. The fastest snake on record was timed at 7 miles (11 kilometers) per hour over a short distance. The harmless racer snakes can equal that speed.

Racers are fast enough to chase and catch smaller snakes and reptiles. Racers are good climbers that can quickly snake up trees and snatch birds' eggs. Racers are fast enough to get out from underfoot. But even at their fastest speed, racers cannot outrun people or many of their predators.

When racers feel threatened, they try to scare off a predator by shaking their tails across dry leaves and plants. This makes a sound like that of a rattlesnake's tail. If that does not scare off a predator, racers will bite.

Racers live in many areas of North America. They are also found in parts of Europe, Africa, and Asia.

Red Racer

Why Do Cobras Look So Frightening?

Cobras *(KOH bruhz)* puff up and hiss in a frightening way to ward off danger. They flatten their long neck ribs, pushing out the skin around their heads to look like hoods. Cobras can even move forward while doing this. It is a very frightening sight!

Puffing and hissing are not all cobras do. Cobras are elapids that use their poison in two different ways. Some cobras bite their prey with their short, immovable fangs. Others spit venom at the eyes of their victims. These "spitting cobras" can spray their venom as far as 8 feet (2.4 meters).

Cobras live in Africa and southern Asia. Most are about 6 feet (1.8 meters) long. King cobras are the largest poisonous snakes in the world. A king cobra can grow to a length of 18 feet (5.5 meters), and its head can be as big as an adult person's hand.

King cobra

Which Snake Will Leave You Breathless?

Pythons *(PY thahnz)* coil their thick bodies around their prey. Then they slowly squeeze the breath out of the animal. Pythons are called constrictors because of the way they suffocate their prey.

Pythons live in southern Asia, Africa, and Australia. Some species are among the largest snakes in the world. They grow to lengths of 20 to 30 feet (6 to 9 meters). But most pythons are much smaller and pose no serious threat to people. In fact, many kinds of pythons are kept as pets. Baby pythons hatch from eggs. Unlike most snakes, a mother python stays with her eggs. Indian pythons and some other python species coil around their eggs to keep them warm until they hatch.

Boas *(BOH uhz)* are also constrictors that can grow to be quite large. Boas are different from pythons in that they give birth to live young.

Diamond python

How Big Is an Anaconda?

Anaconda *(AN uh KAHN duh)* is the name of two well-known kinds of constrictors. One kind is the largest snake in the world. It can grow to be more than 30 feet (9 meters) in length. All adult anacondas are more than 15 feet (4.6 meters) long. An adult snake this size can weigh over 220 pounds (100 kilograms).

These giant snakes live near rivers and other bodies of water in tropical South America. Anacondas are not poisonous. They belong to the boa family of snakes and are often called "water boas." Anacondas prey on turtles, birds, mammals, and small caymans *(KAY muhnz)*—South American crocodiles.

Like most snakes, anacondas are shy. They usually defend themselves from enemies by retreating. If cornered, anacondas will bite. This, along with their great size and weight, can make anacondas dangerous to people.

Anaconda

What Do Snakes Do in the Winter?

Many snakes, such as rattlers and garter snakes, may hibernate, or sleep, during the winter. Why do they do this? In many parts of the world, winter is too cold for snakes. (Remember—snakes are cold-blooded!) They need warmer temperatures to help them keep their bodies working.

As winter approaches, snakes crawl into caves or holes in the ground to escape the cold. Often, many snakes will crowd into a single den to keep warm. Sometimes, more than one species of snake will share a den and sleep through the winter together.

While snakes hibernate, their body temperatures drop, and they stay fairly still. Hibernating snakes use up very little energy and do not have to worry about eating food. When spring arrives, they come out of their dens to warm up and to eat.

Hibernating rattlesnakes

57

What Good Are Snakes?

Snakes do plenty of good things, especially for farmers. Snakes eat mice, rats, gophers, and other small mammals that eat farm crops.

Snakes also help scientists and doctors. Snake venom is used in research and in making medicines. One medicine made from venom helps treat certain types of heart attacks. Another is antivenin (AN tee VEHN uhn), a drug used to treat snakebites!

To collect snake venom, skilled workers must "milk" a poisonous snake. This picture shows how venom drips from the fangs when a snake is milked. To milk a snake, a worker places a cup under the upper jaw of the snake's open mouth. The worker then rubs the snake's venom gland, and the snake shoots venom from its fangs into the cup.

Eastern diamondback
rattlesnake

Are Snakes in Danger?

More than 50 species of snakes are endangered. Part of the reason is that some people eat snakes. Other people wear snakeskin boots, shoes, and belts. Many snakes are overhunted for these reasons.

Some snakes are in danger because of changes to their habitats. This is true for San Francisco garter snakes. As more land is cleared for farms, homes, businesses, and roads, the snakes have fewer places to live.

Many snake deaths happen by mistake. Common water snakes are often killed by people who mistake them for cottonmouths. Some milk snakes are killed because they look a lot like coral snakes. It is true that poisonous snakes are dangerous. But most snakes are not poisonous. Knowing the difference is good for snakes—and for people!

San Francisco
gartersnake

Snake Fun Facts

→ *Sssssnake, Sssserpent,* What's in a name? *Serpent,* another word for *snake,* is often used in myths and legends.

→ Some snakes, like the rubber boa and the African ball python, can roll into a tight ball to protect themselves from predators.

→ In many species, female snakes are larger than males.

→ A popular flag of the Revolutionary War in America (1775–1783) had a picture of a rattlesnake on it. The flag warned: "Don't Tread on Me!"

→ A snake charmer does not actually "charm" a cobra with music. He or she sways back and forth. The snake, following the motions, does the same thing.

→ Snakes can stick out their tongues even when their mouths are closed! The tongue pokes through a small notch on the upper jaw.

Glossary

camouflage Skin colors or patterns that help an animal blend into its habitat.

cold-blooded Having a body temperature that changes with temperature changes in the environment.

elapid A snake belonging to a group of poisonous snakes with short, fixed fangs, as cobras.

fang A long, hollow tooth through which venom flows.

habitat Where an animal lives.

hibernate To sleep through the cold months.

Jacobson's organ A snake's organ of smell, located in the roof of the mouth.

molt To shed skin.

pit organs Heating-sensing organs located on the heads of some snakes between the eyes and nostrils.

predator An animal hunting for food.

prey An animal hunted for food.

reptile A cold-blooded animal with a backbone and scales.

scutes A snake's large belly scales.

venom Snake poison.

vertebrate Any animal having a backbone.

viper A group of poisonous snakes with movable fangs, like rattlesnakes.

Index

(**Boldface** indicates a photo, map, or illustration.)

Picture Acknowledgments: Front & Back Cover: © C. K. Lorenz, Photo Researchers; © Jack Dermid, Photo Researchers; © Jim W. Grace, Photo Researchers; © Joe McDonald, Bruce Coleman Inc.; © Hans Reinhard, Bruce Coleman Inc.

© David Dennis, Tom Stack & Associates 59; © Jack Dermid, Photo Researchers 39; © William J. Weber, Visuals Unlimited 33; © Jeff Foott, Tom Stack & Associates 7, 21; © François Gohier, Photo Researchers 11; © Jim W. Grace, Photo Researchers 41; © Peter B. Kaplan, Photo Researchers 27; © Gary Ladd, Photo Researchers 13; © Jeff Lepore, Photo Researchers 15; © D. J. Lyons, Bruce Coleman Inc. 25; © Steve & David Maslowski, Photo Researchers 43; © Micheal McCoy, Photo Researchers 53; © Joe McDonald, Bruce Coleman Inc. 45; © Joe McDonald, Tom Stack & Associates 4, 17, 47, 51, 61; © Tom McHugh, Photo Researchers 35, 57; © Mark Newman, Tom Stack & Associates 23; © Milton Rand, Tom Stack & Associates 37; © Hans Reinhard, Bruce Coleman Inc. 5, 31; © François Savigny, Animals Animals 55; © Karl H. Switak, Photo Researchers 29, 49.

Illustrations: WORLD BOOK illustration by Michael DiGiorgio 19; WORLD BOOK illustration by Karen Donica 9, 62.